HORSEPOWER

HARLEY-DAVIDSON MOTORCYCLES

by Sarah L. Schuette

Reading Consultant:

Barbara J. Fox

Reading Specialist

North Carolina State University

Capstone
press®

Mankato, Minnesota

Blazers is published by Capstone Press,
151 Good Counsel Drive, P.O. Box 669, Mankato, Minnesota 56002.
www.capstonepress.com

Library of Congress Cataloging-in-Publication Data
Schuette, Sarah L., 1976–
    Harley-Davidson motorcycles / by Sarah L. Schuette.
        p. cm.—(Blazers. Horsepower)
    Summary: "Brief text describes Harley-Davidson motorcycles,
including their main features, how people customize them, and why
they are popular"—Provided by publisher.
    Includes bibliographical references and index.
    ISBN-13: 978-0-7368-6449-7 (hardcover)
    ISBN-10: 0-7368-6449-0 (hardcover)
    1. Harley-Davidson motorcycles—Juvenile literature. I. Title.
II. Series.
    TL448.H3S376 2007
    629.227'5—dc22   2005037735

P796.75

Editorial Credits
Carrie A. Braulick, editor; Jason Knudson, set designer; Thomas
    Emery, book designer; Jo Miller, photo researcher; Scott Thoms,
    photo editor

Photo Credits
Capstone Press/Karon Dubke, cover, 11, 12, 13, 14–15, 16–17, 19,
    20, 21, 23 (both)
Corbis/Ed Kashi, 6–7, 8, 25; Patrick Bennett, 28–29
© 2005 David O. Bailey, 5, 22
Getty Images Inc./AFP Eric Estrade, 26
© 2005 Lauren E. Bailey, 27
UNICORN Stock Photos/Patti McConville, 9

**Capstone Press thanks Harley-Davidson of Mankato, Minnesota, and D & M
Custom Cycle of New Ulm, Minnesota, for their help in preparing this book.**

1 2 3 4 5 6 11 10 09 08 07 06

TABLE OF CONTENTS

RUMBLING TO A RALLY

A pack of Harley-Davidson motorcycles thunders down the highway. Soon, the riders will be at their favorite rally.

Harleys crowd the streets of Sturgis, South Dakota, each summer. Riders visit from around the world.

Whether riders have a classic Harley or a new model, they will receive a warm welcome in Sturgis.

HARLEY DESIGN

The roar of the Harley
V-twin engine can't be ignored.
The engine burns fuel in two
cylinders to give Harleys plenty
of power.

Cylinders

Riders take command of Harleys with handlebar controls. Riders twist the throttle to speed up. Squeezing the front brake slows down the bike.

Front brake

Throttle

To shift gears, riders use a foot control. They lift up or push down on the gear lever.

Gear lever

GREVE

Large exhaust pipes make the Harley's famous rumbling sound heard. They also keep the engine cool.

Exhaust pipes

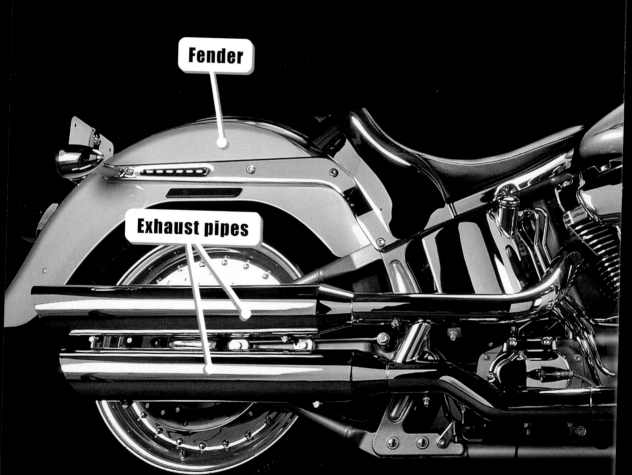

HARLEY PARTS

Fender

Exhaust pipes

Throttle

Front brake

Gas tank

Fork

Fender

Engine cylinders

A CUSTOM LOOK

Some Harley riders change their bikes to show their own style. New paint jobs, shiny chrome parts, and long forks give bikes a custom look.

Fork

Some riders replace nearly all of the original Harley parts with custom parts. These bikes look almost nothing like the factory models.

BLAZER FACT

Some Harleys have custom air filters. Builders redesign the filter shapes and paint them.

Air filters

Some Harley riders enjoy cruising on three wheels. Sidecars on Harleys let another person come along for the ride. Bikes can be made into stylish trikes.

BLAZER FACT

Most sidecars have a design and color that matches the motorcycle.

Trike

THE OPEN ROAD

Riding in groups or cruising alone, Harley-Davidsons remain one of the most loved motorcycles of all time.

Adventure and freedom draw riders to Harley-Davidsons. Riders live to rumble down the open road.

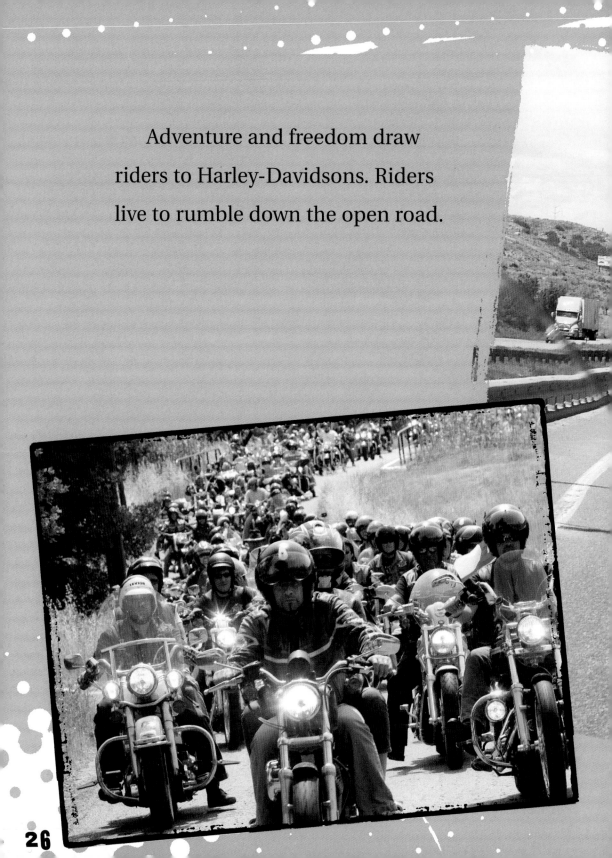

BLAZER FACT

Harley-Davidson is the most popular U.S. motorcycle company. The Harley Owners Group (H.O.G.) has almost 1 million members.

HEADING OUT ON THE HIGHWAY!

GLOSSARY

chrome (KHROME)—a shiny metallic coating on a motorcycle part

cylinder (SIL-uhn-dur)—a hollow chamber inside an engine where fuel burns to create power

factory model (FAK-tuh-ree MOD-uhl)—a motorcycle that has all of the parts that were installed at the factory

fork (FORK)—the motorcycle part that holds the front tire

rally (RAL-ee)—a large meeting of motorcycle riders

throttle (THROT-uhl)—the vehicle part that controls how much fuel and air flow into an engine; motorcycle riders twist the throttle to speed up.

READ MORE

Kimber, David, and Richard Newland. *Motorcycle-Mania!* Vehicle-Mania! Milwaukee: Gareth Stevens, 2004.

Preszler, Eric. *Harley-Davidson Motorcycles.* Wild Rides! Mankato, Minn.: Capstone Press, 2004.

Sherman, Josepha. *The Story of Harley-Davidson.* A Robbie Reader. Hockessin, Del.: Mitchell Lane, 2005.

INTERNET SITES

FactHound offers a safe, fun way to find Internet sites related to this book. All of the sites on FactHound have been researched by our staff.

Here's how:

1. Visit *www.facthound.com*

2. Choose your grade level.

3. Type in this book ID **0736864490** for age-appropriate sites. You may also browse subjects by clicking on letters, or by clicking on pictures and words.

4. Click on the **Fetch It** button.

FactHound will fetch the best sites for you!

INDEX